How to Use This

The **Teaching Versions** of *Elements of Reading: Fluency* will help you guide students to become fluent readers. Because fluency is not an isolated skill but is closely linked to word knowledge and comprehension, each **Teaching Version** contains the following types of teacher support:

- **Fluency teaching suggestions** to help students become proficient in reading with expression (prosody).

- **Word knowledge teaching suggestions** to build students' proficiency in reading words and understanding their structure and meanings. The word knowledge suggestions address high-frequency words, decoding skills, structural analysis skills, and knowledge of word meanings.

- **Sentence comprehension questions** to help students develop literal comprehension at the sentence level.

- **Story comprehension questions** to help students develop inferential comprehension. Additional comprehension questions are provided in the **Teacher's Lesson Folder**.

After students complete the repeated reading activity outlined on page 4.8 of the **Teacher's Lesson Folder**, use the reduced **Student Book** pages and teaching suggestions in this **Teaching Version** to provide explicit page-by-page instruction.

The Rat Princess

■ **Fluency Focus**

Expression Conveying feelings, mood, or characterization

Punctuation Observing junctures indicated by commas

Text Format Reading a play

Text Format Understanding that italicized words often convey emphasis.

■ **Word Knowledge Focus**

Decoding Words with silent *gh*

High-Frequency Words (Boldface words appear in each book of the theme.)

a, all, am, and, are, around, as, ask, asked, at, away, be, **been,** best, better, big, but, call, can, come, day, do, don't, down, earth, every, father, feel, find, for, found, go, goes, going, great, grow, hard, have, he, help, him, home, hot, **hurt**, I, **important**, in, is, it, just, kind, know, land, let, life, **light**, like, little, long, make, may, me, more, most, move, much, must, my, need, never, no, not, now, of, off, on, one, only, or, out, over, **picked**, please, really, right, say, **second**, see, shall, show, so, some, something, **start**, still, tell, than, thank, that, the, them, then, there, these, thing, think, time, to, too, up, us, very, want, warm, **was**, wash, we, what, who, will, with, would, yes, you

■ **Sentence Comprehension Focus**

Identifying character feelings

■ **Story Comprehension Focus**

Identifying character traits

The Rat Princess

Written by Michaela Morgan
Illustrated by Emma Garner

Harcourt
Supplemental Publishers
Rigby • Steck-Vaughn

www.steck-vaughn.com

Getting Started

To begin, invite a volunteer to read the title page aloud.

Book Summary

In this play, Rat Princess asks her father to help her choose a husband. The princess wants a husband who is kind and gentle, but the king thinks she should marry someone very powerful. After interviewing some powerful candidates, Rat Princess discovers that Gray Rat is just what she is looking for.

Ask students what kind of fiction the book is and how they can tell (a play; the characters are listed on the page). Invite students to read the characters' names aloud.

Characters

RAT PRINCESS

RAT KING

HOT SUN

RAIN CLOUD

SWIFT WIND

GREAT WALL

GRAY RAT

Scene 1

RAT PRINCESS: I want to ask you something important, Father.

RAT KING: Dear daughter, ask for anything, and you shall have it. Ask for anything at all—gold, silver, cheese—.

RAT PRINCESS: Father, I want to marry. Will you help me pick a husband?

RAT KING: You want to marry? Yes, I will help you pick a husband. You are beautiful and important, so I will help you pick the best husband in the land.

3

■ Sentence Comprehension

Ask *What is Rat King's reason for helping his daughter pick the best husband in the land?* (She is beautiful and important.)

■ Fluency

Point out the character name at the beginning of each block of text. Explain that a play is set up so that it is easy for each character to know when he or she speaks and exactly what to say. Tell students that when a play is read aloud or performed, only the characters' words are read.

Read the first two blocks of text aloud. Read the dialogue for Rat Princess in a high, sweet voice and the dialogue for Rat King in a deep, regal voice. Call attention to the commas on the page. Remind students that commas usually signal a brief pause.

Point out the dashes and explain that a reader should also pause briefly for them.

■ Word Knowledge

Have a volunteer write the theme high-frequency words *hurt, important, light, picked, second, start,* and *was* on the board. Invite students to read them aloud with you. Then ask students to find the word *important* on the page.

■ Fluency

Direct students' attention to the first block of text. Ask students where they should pause when reading Rat Princess' words (after "father," "kind," and "me").

Tell students that a fluent reader thinks about what the characters are like, what they are saying, and how people sound when they say those things in conversation. Have students read the page silently to decide how Rat Princess' and Rat King's words should be read to convey their personality and feelings. Have volunteers read aloud character parts of their choice to demonstrate their interpretation.

RAT PRINCESS: Father, I want a kind, gentle husband who wants to marry me, too.

RAT KING: Oh, no, dear daughter. It is more important that you pick someone who is very, very powerful.

RAT PRINCESS: The husband I will pick must have beautiful eyes. He must have soft paws and fine whiskers!

RAT KING: Beautiful eyes! Soft paws! Fine whiskers! These are not important things. You need a powerful husband. Let's start at the top. We'll ask Hot Sun. He is big, and he is bright. And he's right up there.

4

■ Sentence Comprehension

Ask *What kind of husband does Rat Princess want?* (one with beautiful eyes, soft paws, and fine whiskers)

■ Word Knowledge

Have students read aloud the list of theme high-frequency words on the board. Ask students which words appear on page 4.

Direct students' attention to the word "bright." Write the word on the board and discuss with students the silent *gh* combination. Ask students to identify the word in the last sentence that has silent *gh* ("right"). Invite students to think of other words that rhyme with "bright" and "right." Have a volunteer write the ones with silent *gh* on the board. Tell students they will come across more words with silent *gh* as they go through the play.

■ Fluency

Ask students who Rat Princess talks to in the first sentence (Hot Sun). Explain the purpose of the comma after "Hot Sun"—to indicate that Hot Sun is being spoken to (direct address). Have students find other instances of direct address on the page (in the third text block).

Invite volunteers to read the character parts aloud. Encourage them to "be the character."

Scene 2

RAT PRINCESS: Hot Sun, we want to ask you something.

HOT SUN: Ask me anything.

RAT KING: Hot Sun, Hot Sun, Rat King and Princess have come to call. Tell us, Hot Sun, are you the most powerful one of all?

HOT SUN: What was that you asked? Am I the most powerful one of all? Let me think. Yes, I think I am! Nothing can hurt mighty me! I'm as mighty as mighty can be!

RAT PRINCESS: Oh, no! I don't think I want to marry Hot Sun. He'll burn my fur.

6

■ Sentence Comprehension

Ask *Why doesn't Rat Princess want to marry Hot Sun?* (because he will burn her fur)

7

Ask students which of the theme high-frequency words appear on page 6.

Have students find the word on page 6 that has silent *gh* ("mighty").

■ Fluency

Discuss with students how each character is feeling at this point in the plot. Have volunteers use this knowledge to read the page aloud with expression that conveys the feelings.

Point out the italicized "*me*" and guide students to connect its form with its function—to convey emphasis.

HOT SUN: I am mighty. I am powerful. I warm the earth. I light the sky to start the day. I make plants and flowers grow. And the earth goes around *me!* I call that powerful!

RAT KING: You are very powerful indeed!

RAT PRINCESS: Oh, Father. I don't think I want to marry Hot Sun. He'll burn my whiskers.

8

■ Sentence Comprehension

Ask *Why does Hot Sun say he is the most powerful?* (because he warms the earth, lights the sky to start the day, makes plants and flowers grow, and the earth goes around him)

RAT KING: But are you the *most* powerful one of all?

HOT SUN: Wait one second. There *is* one thing more powerful than I am.

RAT KING: What is it?

RAT PRINCESS: What is it?

HOT SUN: It's Rain Cloud. Rain Cloud blocks me out, so Rain Cloud is much more powerful than I am.

9

■ Sentence Comprehension

Ask *What does Hot Sun say is more powerful than he is?* (Rain Cloud)

■ Fluency

Have students find the italicized words on the page and read aloud the sentences containing them. Encourage students to stress the italicized words to convey emphasis.

Then read the page aloud in a disfluent manner: read in a fast monotone with no pauses. Have students tell how your reading could have been better.

■ Word Knowledge

Have students read aloud the list of theme high-frequency words on the board. Ask them to find the ones that appear on pages 8–9.

Direct students' attention to the word "mighty" on page 8. Ask students which letters in the word are silent (*gh*). Then ask which theme high-frequency word has silent *gh* (*light*).

■ Fluency

Invite students to read along with you in a choral reading of the page. Before reading, discuss how Rat King probably feels (happy and excited because he thinks he has solved a problem). Also point out the rhyming words "best" and "rest" and suggest that emphasizing the words slightly will help a listener hear the rhyme.

RAT KING: Yes! Rain Cloud blocks out Hot Sun, so Rain Cloud is more powerful than Hot Sun. Rain Cloud is the biggest. Rain Cloud is the best. Rain Cloud is better than all the rest! And he's just over there.

10

■ Sentence Comprehension

Ask *Why is Rain Cloud more powerful than Hot Sun?* (He can block out Hot Sun.)

Scene 3

RAT PRINCESS: Hello, Rain Cloud. We have come to ask you something.

RAIN CLOUD: Hello. What is it you want? Ask me anything. Would you like some rain?

RAT PRINCESS: Not just now, thank you.

RAT KING: Rain Cloud, Rain Cloud, Rat King and Princess have come to call. Tell us, Rain Cloud, are you the most powerful one of all?

11

■ Sentence Comprehension

Ask *What does Rain Cloud think Rat Princess wants?* (some rain)

■ Fluency

Direct students' attention to Rat King's words at the bottom of the page. Ask students to whom Rat King is talking (Rain Cloud). Call on volunteers to demonstrate how Rat King's words should be read to convey his personality and feelings and emphasize the rhyming words "call" and "all."

Assign volunteers the character parts on the page and have them perform a dramatic reading.

■ Word Knowledge

Draw students' attention to the word "mighty." Write the word on the board. Invite a volunteer to circle the silent letters in the word (*gh*).

■ Fluency

Read Rain Cloud's words aloud in a haughty manner. Ask students if your reading matched Rain Cloud's personality. Remind students that in a play, actors become the characters, and they read their lines in ways that show how the characters feel or what they believe.

Have students decide how Rat Princess feels about Rain Cloud. Call on volunteers to read Rat Princess' lines and have the class comment on their reading.

RAIN CLOUD: What was that you asked? Am I the most powerful one of all? Let me think. Yes, I am powerful! I can block out Hot Sun. I can rain on everyone. Nothing can hurt mighty me! I'm as mighty as mighty can be.

RAT PRINCESS: Oh, no! Rain Cloud looks very gray and gloomy. He's so dim! I don't think I want to marry him.

12

■ Sentence Comprehension

Ask *Why does Rain Cloud think he is the most powerful?* (because he can block out Hot Sun, and he can rain on everyone)

RAT KING: But are you the *most* powerful one
of all?

RAIN CLOUD: Wait just one second . There *is* one
thing more powerful than I am. It's Swift
Wind. Swift Wind blows me away, so Swift
Wind is more powerful than I am.

RAT KING: Ah, yes! Swift Wind. Swift Wind is
the biggest. Swift Wind is the best! Swift
Wind is better than all the rest! And he's
just over there!

13

■ Fluency

Invite volunteers to read the
parts of Rain Cloud and Rat
King. Encourage volunteers
to read their parts with
feeling.

■ Word Knowledge

Ask students to find the theme
high-frequency words on
pages 12 and 13.

Then have students identify
the word with a silent conso-
nant *gh* ("mighty").

■ Sentence Comprehension

Ask   *According to Rain Cloud
and Rat King, who is
more powerful than Rain
Cloud?* (Swift Wind)

■ Fluency

Read the first block of text aloud, pausing at the comma. Ask students why you paused there. (The comma indicates direct address.)

Then read the words of Swift Wind devoid of expression. Ask students if they think this is how Swift Wind sounds. Invite a volunteer to read Swift Wind's words correctly.

Scene 4

RAT PRINCESS: Swift Wind, can you stay still for just a second? There is something we want to ask you.

SWIFT WIND: Whoosh! I can't stay still for long! That's not what I do! Whoosh! I'm the wild, wild wind. I rush and I whoosh. I whirl and I swirl. Whoosh!

RAT PRINCESS: Oh, I don't think I want to marry Swift Wind. I would never have a quiet life with him around!

RAT KING: Swift Wind, Swift Wind, Rat King and Princess have come to call. Tell us, Swift Wind, are you the most powerful one of all?

14

■ Sentence Comprehension

Ask *Why doesn't Rat Princess want to marry Swift Wind?* (She would never have a quiet life with him around.)

SWIFT WIND: What was that you asked? Am I the most powerful one of all? I would say so! I can blow away Rain Cloud. I can whisper and whistle and scream out loud. I can start big waves in the seas. I can make a light and gentle breeze. Nothing can hurt mighty me! I'm as mighty as mighty can be!

15

■ Fluency

Lead students to conclude that Swift Wind has a high opinion of himself and is very arrogant. Ask students how they think Swift Wind would sound. Invite a volunteer to read Swift Wind's words in a proud and haughty manner.

■ Word Knowledge

Have students find the theme high-frequency words on pages 14–15.

■ Sentence Comprehension

Ask *Why does Swift Wind say he is the most powerful?* (He can blow away Rain Cloud; whisper and whistle and scream out loud; start big waves in the seas; make a light and gentle breeze; and nothing can hurt him.)

RAT PRINCESS: But isn't there *anything* that can stand up to you?

SWIFT WIND: Wait just one second . There *is* something stronger than I am. I've been huffing and puffing at Great Wall for a long time now, but it still stands. Great Wall stands up to me, so Great Wall is stronger than I am.

16

■ Word Knowledge

Have students read aloud the list of theme high-frequency words on the board. Ask them to find the one that appears on the page. Invite a volunteer to read aloud the sentence containing the word.

■ Sentence Comprehension

Ask *Why does Swift Wind think that Great Wall is stronger than he is?* (because Great Wall stands up to him)

RAT KING: Great Wall is the biggest. Great Wall is the best. Great Wall is better than all the rest. Off we go to see Great Wall!

RAT PRINCESS: I don't think I want to marry a wall. A wall doesn't have beautiful eyes, soft paws, and fine whiskers.

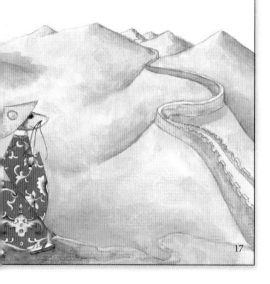

17

■ Fluency

Divide the class into three groups. Assign each group a character part. Have the groups rehearse their part and peform it chorally. Remind groups to pause appropriately for commas.

■ Sentence Comprehension

Ask Why doesn't Rat Princess want to marry a wall? (because a wall doesn't have beautiful eyes, soft paws, and fine whiskers)

■ Fluency

Ask students to speculate on the feelings of each character. Point out that Rat Princess has already said she doesn't want to marry a wall, so her lines should not be read cheerfully or hopefully.

Lead students in a choral reading of the page that conveys the feelings of each character.

■ Word Knowledge

Have students read aloud the list of theme high-frequency words on the board. Ask them to find the ones that appear on the page. Invite volunteers to read aloud the sentences containing the words.

Scene 5

RAT PRINCESS: Great Wall, may we ask you something?

GREAT WALL: What is it you want to know?

RAT KING: Great Wall, Great Wall, Rat King and Princess have come to call. Tell us, Great Wall, are you the most powerful one of all?

GREAT WALL: What was that you asked? Am I the most powerful one of all? I would say so! Swift Wind can't move me. Hot Sun can't melt me. Rain Cloud can't wash me away. Nothing can hurt mighty me! I am mighty as mighty as can be!

18

■ Sentence Comprehension

Ask *According to Great Wall, why is he the most powerful one of all?* (Swift Wind can't move him; Hot Sun can't melt him; Rain Cloud can't wash him away; nothing can hurt him.)

RAT PRINCESS: I don't think I want to marry Great Wall. He is too hard! I want a kind, gentle husband, with beautiful eyes, soft paws, and fine whiskers. Father, I really don't want to marry a wall. Please help me find the best husband.

GREAT WALL: Mighty, mighty me! I'm as mighty as mighty can be. But there *is* one thing stronger than I am.

19

■ Fluency

Read the page without expression of any kind and without pausing for commas or end punctuation. Ask students how your reading could have been better. Invite students to demonstrate a better reading. Encourage them to convey Rat Princess' growing sense of desperation and Great Wall's emphasis on "is."

■ Sentence Comprehension

Ask *Why doesn't Rat Princess want to marry Great Wall?* (because he is too hard)

■ Fluency

Ask students to read Rat Princess' second bit of dialogue and describe how Rat Princess feels at this point in the play (discouraged). Guide students to conclude that Rat King still is hopeful that they will find the perfect husband for her.

Invite volunteers to read the parts of Rat King, Rat Princess, and Great Wall. Remind volunteers to read their parts as though the characters are speaking.

RAT KING: What is it?

RAT PRINCESS: What is it?

GREAT WALL: Something keeps nibbling away at me. I feel a little bit of me going every day. It's something deep down at my foot. I don't know what it is, but it must be very powerful.

RAT KING: We must find it! Then we will have found the most powerful one of all. Then, dear daughter, you will have picked the best husband there is.

RAT PRINCESS: Will it be as hard as Great Wall? Will it be as loud as Swift Wind? Will it be as gloomy as Rain Cloud? Or will it be as hot as Hot Sun? What will it be?

RAT KING: Hello, hello, you who are best of all. Rat King and Princess have come to call. You are more powerful than Great Wall. Come out and show us the most powerful one of all!

20

■ Sentence Comprehension

Ask *According to Great Wall, what is more powerful than he is?* (something that keeps nibbling at his foot)

21

■ Word Knowledge

Have students read aloud the list of theme high-frequency words on the board. Ask them to find the one that appears on page 20. Invite a volunteer to read aloud the sentence containing the word.

■ Fluency

Divide the class into two groups. Assign each group a character part. Have the groups rehearse the parts and perform them chorally. Remind groups to pause appropriately for commas.

GRAY RAT: I am not the most powerful one of all. I am only a little gray rat. Please come in and rest. You must be tired. I will make some tea for you.

RAT PRINCESS: Oh, Gray Rat, you are kind and gentle. And what beautiful eyes, soft paws, and fine whiskers you have! You are the rat for me!

22

■ Sentence Comprehension

Ask *Who is the most powerful one of all?* (Gray Rat)

RAT KING: I would not have picked Gray Rat for you, dear daughter. But he is better than all the rest.

RAT PRINCESS: Oh, Father. I have picked the very best husband in the land.

RAT KING: Then, dear daughter, you will have the best wedding in the land, too.

23

■ Sentence Comprehension

Ask *Why does Rat Princess say that Gray Rat is the best husband in the land?* (because he is kind and gentle and has beautiful eyes, soft paws, and fine whiskers)

■ Fluency

Point out the comma in the final text block. Ask students what the comma signals (a brief pause) and why it is there. (Rat King is addressing his daughter.) Ask two students to read the parts of Rat King and Rat Princess as if talking to each other.

■ Word Knowledge

Have students read aloud the list of theme high-frequency words on the board. Ask them to find the one that appears on page 20. Invite volunteers to read aloud the sentences containing the word.

■ Fluency

Invite students to read along with you in a choral reading of the page.

HOT SUN: My wedding gift to you will be a bright and sunny day.

RAIN CLOUD: My gift to you will be some lovely and cool shade.

SWIFT WIND: My gift to you will be a light and gentle breeze.

GREAT WALL: My gift to you will be a home that will stand tall forever.

RAT PRINCESS: Thank you. But the best gift of all will be the love of my gentle Gray Rat. In any kind of weather, I will be happy with that.

24

■ Sentence Comprehension

Ask *What does Rat Princess think is the best wedding gift of all?* (Gray Rat)

■ Story Comprehension

Ask   *How are Hot Sun, Rain Cloud, Swift Wind, and Great Wall alike?* (They are arrogant and proud.)

Ask   *How does Rat King feel about Hot Sun, Rain Cloud, Swift Wind, and Great Wall?* (He is impressed by all of them; he thinks they are all powerful and would be right for his daughter.)

Ask   *How does Rat Princess feel about Hot Sun, Rain Cloud, Swift Wind, and Great Wall?* (She doesn't like any of them.)

RAT PRINCESS: Hot Sun, we want to ask you something. — 7, 8

HOT SUN: Ask me anything. — 11

RAT KING: Hot Sun, Hot Sun, Rat King and Princess have come to call. Tell us, Hot Sun, are you the most powerful one of all? — 18, 26, 35

HOT SUN: What was that you asked? Am I the most powerful one of all? Let me think. Yes, I think I am! Nothing can hurt mighty me! I'm as mighty as mighty can be! — 43, 51, 60, 68

RAT PRINCESS: Oh, no! I don't think I want to marry Hot Sun. He'll burn my fur. — 76, 83

HOT SUN: I am mighty. I am powerful. I warm the earth. I light the sky to start the day. I make plants and flowers grow. And the earth goes around *me!* I call that powerful! — 91, 102, 109, 117

RAT KING: You are very powerful indeed! — 122

RAT PRINCESS: Oh, Father. I don't think I want to marry Hot Sun. He'll burn my whiskers. — 130, 137

RAT KING: But are you the *most* powerful one of all? — 144, 146

HOT SUN: Wait one second. There *is* one thing more powerful than I am. — 153, 158

RAT KING: What is it? — 161

RAT PRINCESS: What is it? — 164

HOT SUN: It's Rain Cloud. Rain Cloud blocks me out, so Rain Cloud is much more powerful than I am. — 171, 179, 182

■ Fluency Flip Page

The **Fluency Flip Page** of the **Student Book** contains a passage from the book to facilitate timed reading. For more information on timed reading and other ways of assessing fluency, see the **Teacher's Lesson Folder**.